YOTSUBA&!

7

KIYOHIKO AZUMA

CONTENTS

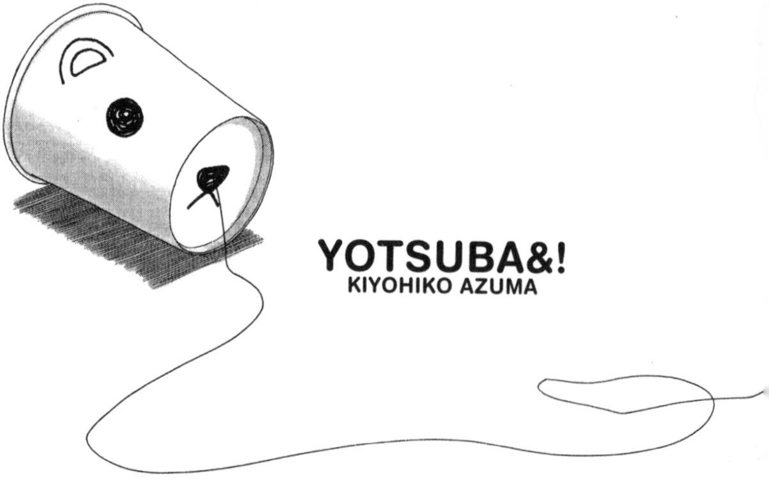

YOTSUBA&!

KIYOHIKO AZUMA

YOTSUBA&
TELEPHONES!
#42

OKAY, NOW WALK AWAY FROM ME.
GO DOWN THE STAIRS.
A LITTLE MORE, UNTIL THE STRING IS TIGHT.

NOW PUT THE CUP UP TO YOUR EAR.
NO, I MEAN THE OPEN PART.
?
HELLO?
!

HELLO, CAN YOU HEAR ME?
!
?
HELLO?
IF YOU CAN HEAR ME, RAISE YOUR RIGHT HAND.
SA (SHWP)
!
PUT YOUR RIGHT HAND DOWN.
SA
NOW IF YOU CAN HEAR ME, TAKE YOUR RIGHT HAND AND...
... DON'T RAISE IT.
SA

!?
SA
SA
AH-HA-HA-HA! YOU CAN HEAR ME.
COOL!
ENA!
A VOICE COME FROM THIS CUP!
IF YOU TALK INTO IT, I'LL BE ABLE TO HEAR YOU TOO.
I HEARED YOUR VOICE, ENA.
DID YOU HEAR ME!? DID YOU HEAR ME!?
PUT THE CUP UP TO YOUR EAR.

I HEARD YOU!
WHAT ARE YOU DOING?
OH! IT'S MIURA.
MIURA IS HERE.
I CAN SEE THAT.
HUH, SO EVEN ENA DOES KIDDY THINGS SOME-TIMES...
THIS CUP TURNED INTO A CELL PHONE!
YOU'RE GOING TO CARRY IT AROUND? GUESS IT'LL BE PRETTY USEFUL IF YOU WANT TO DRINK SOME-THING.
RIGHT!
DOES MIURA HAVE A CELL PHONE?
NO, BUT I WANT ONE.

*-NEECHAN: AN INFORMAL HONORIFIC SUFFIX USED TO ADDRESS AN OLDER SISTER OR AN UNRELATED YOUNG WOMAN WHO IS OLDER THAN THE SPEAKER.

ASAGIIIII!
AAAA-SAAA-GIIIIII!
WHAT?
CALL FOR YOU!
HELLO, ASAGI? CAN YOU HEAR YOTSUBA?

HELLO, ASAGI? CAN YOU HEAR YOTSUBA?
!
IT'S YOTSUBA. I BOUGHT A NEW CELL PHONE.
HUH?
IT'S YOTSUBA. I BOUGHT A NEW CELL PHONE.
!
THE STRING IS MESSED UP!
NEXT TIME, I'LL SEND YOU AN E-MAIL.
IT CAME!
THIS LOOKS LIKE FUN! I WANNA MAKE ONE TOO!

*AU: A JAPANESE CELL PHONE BRAND. THE NAME IS BASED ON THE JAPANESE WORD FOR "TO MEET."

I WONDER IF OUR VOICES WILL STOP AT THE KNOT?
LET'S TRY IT.
WILL IT WORK IF WE TIE THE STRINGS TOGETHER LIKE THIS?
KEEP GOING UNTIL THE STRING IS TIGHT.
YOTSUBA, YOU GO TO THE KITCHEN.

*-CHAN: AN INFORMAL HONORIFIC SUFFIX USED WHEN REFERRING TO CHILDREN AND YOUNG GIRLS THAT EXPRESSES FAMILIARITY.

HMM...
だだだ
DA DA DA
(THD-D-D)
がらっ
GARA
(CLATTER)
?

HUH?
WHAT?
CAN WE USE YOUR WINDOW?
WE'RE GOING TO RUN A PHONE LINE OVER TO YOTSUBA'S HOUSE.
HUH?

HOW DO WE GET IT OVER THERE? I GUESS WE HAVE TO THROW IT.
BUT IT'S TOO LIGHT. IT WON'T REACH.
MAYBE ADD WEIGHT TO IT?
SOMETHING HEAVY MIGHT BREAK THE WINDOW, THOUGH.
HMM... YOU'RE RIGHT...
56
FUUKA-NEECHAN, I'M GOING TO BORROW THIS STUFFED ANIMAL.
UM, OKAY?
よつば
12
CUP: YOTSUBA

ALL RIGHT.
WHA !?
HYUN (FWOOSH)
?
TRY IT AGAIN!

GOT IT!
A STRING PHONE, HUH?
HELLO? THIS IS YOTSUBA.
HEY, IT'S ME.
YEAH.
HUH!?
YEAH.
...UH-HUH.
DADDY GOT CAUGHT BY POLICE...
...AND IF WE DON'T PAY MONEY...
THAT'S A SCAM!

YOTSUBA, WE HAVE SNACKS.
BE RIGHT THERE!
YOTSUBA HAS THIS, SO SHE DOESN'T EVEN HAVE TO GO NEXT DOOR, RIGHT !?
YOU DON'T WANT TO GO OVER THERE?
POI (TOSS)
ぽい
ZUZU (SLIDE)
ずずっ
HASHI (CATCH)
はしっ
I'LL STICK IT IN HERE.
ば45

DA DA DA
(THD-D-D)
WHAT'S FOR SNACKS?
DOUGHNUTS.

HELLO?
CAN YOU HEAR ME?
YEAH, RIGHT.
YES, I CAN HEAR YOU.
!
OH! I'M SORRY.
I DIDN'T THINK SOMEONE WOULD PICK UP.
86 kcal

OUR VOICES COME THROUGH PRETTY CLEAR ON THESE, HUH?
YEAH.
IS YOTSUBA-CHAN IN HERE?
HEY.
IT'S NOT WHAT IT LOOKS LIKE!

YOU'VE GOT THE WRONG IDEA!
THEN WHAT IS GOING ON HERE?
OH.
THIS IS PERFECT.
COULD I BORROW THAT FOR A SEC?
HUH?
UH, HELLO.
OH?
TORAKO JUST FINISHED PRINTING THE PICTURES SHE TOOK.
I'LL SEND THEM TO YOU LATER.
BY E-MAIL.
E-MAIL?

E-MAIL?
THAT'S RIGHT.
STARTING RIGHT NOW, YOU'RE E-MAIL.
......I UNDER-STAND.
YOU DO? THOSE ARE SOME POWERS OF COMPRE-HENSION YOU'VE GOT.
TURN YOUR BACK TOWARD ME.
PICTURES, ATTACHED!
SFX: BETAN (STICK)
GIVE THOSE TO YOUR DAD, OKAY?
OKAY.
YO-TSUBA'S E-MAIL.
HEY YOTSUBA, SINCE YOU'RE E-MAIL, YOU NEED TO HAVE AN EMOTICON.

DADDY! E-MAIL!
SO YOU WERE E-MAIL, HUH?
YUP.
I WONDER WHAT KIND OF PICTURES SHE GOT.
......
WHAT'S WITH THAT FACE?

YOTSUBA&!

YOTSUBA&!

RESPECT FOR THE AGED DAY

#43

!
DADDY!
ばん
BAN (WHACK)
KAAAAAAH!!
NOT THAT!
MAKE A PHONE CALL!
A PHONE CALL !?
ぱっ
BA (SNATCH)

HERE'S WHAT I THINK OF YOUR PHONE CALL!!
GASU (WHAM)
GYAAAAAH!!
...AND?
WHY A PHONE CALL ALL OF A SUDDEN?
WHO DO YOU WANT TO CALL?
GRANDMA!
GRANDMA?
THAT'S OKAY... BUT WHY?
HURRY, HURRY!
?

プルルルル
BURURURURU
(BRIIIIING)
プルルルル
BURURURURU
ガチャ
GACHA
(GCHACK)
AH.
HELLO? IT'S ME.
YEAH.
YEAH, I'M FINE.
YEAH.
YEAH, I'M OKAY.
HUH?
NO, HASN'T BEEN HERE AT ALL.
YEAH. I DUNNO.
LET ME HAVE IT!
LET ME HAVE IT!
OH.
YOTSUBA WANTS TO TALK TO YOU.
YEAH.
HURRY!

*RESPECT FOR THE AGED DAY IS A NATIONAL HOLIDAY IN JAPAN. ON THE THIRD MONDAY OF SEPTEMBER, SPECIAL CEREMONIES ARE HELD TO HONOR THE ELDERLY.

CALENDAR: RESPECT FOR THE AGED DAY

YOTSUBA RIDED A BIKE TO GO SHOPPING!
WITH DADDY.
A BIKE CAN EVEN GO TO BIG PLACES!
RIGHT!
BOX: YOTSUBOX
YOTSUBA DOESN'T HAVE A LICENSE YET, SO...
HUH?
A LICENSE!
YOU KNOW, A LICENSE!
ピンポーン
PINPOON (DING-DOONG)
HN?
YO-TSU-BA-CHAN.
OH.
IT'S ENA. TIME TO END THE PHONE CALL.
GRANDMA, ENA'S HERE!
GOTTA GO!
BYE! TALK TO YOU LATER!

I'M GOING TO GO TO MIURA-CHAN'S HOUSE, AND THEN WE'RE GOING TO GO TO THE SCHOOL TOGETHER.
WE'RE GOING TO PLAY IN THE SCHOOL YARD.
OH!
YOU'RE GOING ON YOUR BIKE?
YES.
WHY DON'T YOU COME WITH US ON YOUR BIKE?
I'LL ASK DADDY!
THE ELEMENTARY SCHOOL, HUH?
WELL, IT'S CLOSE, AND YOU'LL BE WITH ENA-CHAN, SO IT'S OKAY.
YAY!!

DRIVE SAFELY AND OBEY THE TRAFFIC RULES ...
...JUST LIKE YOU DID WHEN YOU WENT SHOPPING WITH ME.
UNDER-STOOP!
...WHAT DOES THAT MEAN?
YOTSUBA JUST THOUGHT OF IT.
WHATEVER. OKAY, ENA-CHAN, YOU'LL BE HER INSTRUCTOR FOR TODAY.
HUH? INSTRUCTOR?
RIGHT. IF SHE RIDES STRANGELY, SCOLD HER FOR IT.
TEACH HER HOW TO DRIVE SAFELY.
O-OKAY!
ALL RIGHT, THEN, SEE YOU GUYS LATER.
BE CAREFUL.
UNDER-STOOP!
AH-HA-HA-HA-HA! AH-HA-HA-HA-HA!
WHAT DOES THAT MEAN ...?

HOW'S YOTSU-BA'S DRIV-ING?
SAFE?
PLEASE LOOK WHERE YOU'RE GOING.
ガラ ガラ ガラ
SFX: GARA (CLATTER) GARA GARA
RIGHT.
OKAY, STOP!

*THE FIRST PART OF THE WORD ON THE STREET IS WRITTEN AS A CHINESE CHARACTER, WHICH CHILDREN LEARN IN SCHOOL, SO YOTSUBA CAN'T READ IT YET. BUT SHE CAN READ THE LAST PART OF THE WORD, WHICH IS WRITTEN IN SIMPLER JAPANESE LETTERS. SHE INCORRECTLY GUESSES THAT IT SAYS, "MARUMARE" (CURL INTO A BALL) INSTEAD OF "TOMARE" (STOP).

WRONG!
IT SAYS "STOP AHEAD"!
OHHH—
YOU HAVE TO STOP AT THIS LINE.
THAT'S THE RULE?
DADDY SAID TO STOP WHEN WE COME TO A CROSS-ROAD.
AT THIS LINE?

OH.
PHONE LINES.
THOSE GO ALL THE WAY TO GRANDMA'S HOUSE, RIGHT?
HUH? WAIT, THE PHONE AT YOTSUBA'S HOUSE DOESN'T HAVE A LINE.
OKAY, HERE WE ARE.
がら GARA
がら GARA
がら GARA (CLATTER)

I'M HERE.
OKAY, BE DOWN IN A SEC.

GAAA (GSSSHHH)
THANKS FOR WAITING.
IT'S AUTO-MATIC!
EVEN THOUGH IT'S A HOUSE...
OH, YOTSUBA'S HERE TOO, HUH?
MIURA'S HOUSE IS HUGE!
ARE YOU A PRIN-CESS!?
YES.
I'VE BEEN HIDING IT, BUT I'M ACTUALLY A PRINCESS.
WHOA—

LISTEN, DON'T TELL ANYONE, OKAY?
SHHH!
IT'S A SECRET.
OKAY... UNDER-STOOD.
UNDER-STOOP!!
HUH!?
WHAT DOES THAT MEAN!?
NIIIII (GRIIIN)
WHAT?
I KNOW.
I KNOW THAT.
OH, YOU KNOW WHAT THIS IS?

HUH!?
WRONG.
IT'S A FOLDING BICYCLE!
!
YOU GET ON LIKE THIS.
OHHH!!

WHY IS THERE ONLY ONE WHEEL!?
UMM...
BECAUSE I DON'T HAVE ANY MONEY. I COULD ONLY BUY ONE.
OH, I SEE...
EVEN THOUGH YOU'RE A PRINCESS ...
REALITY IS HARSH, RIGHT?
YOU'VE GOT THAT RIGHT.
OKAY, LET'S GO TO THE SCHOOL.
IT'S DANGEROUS TO RIDE AROUND HERE.
OKAY.
UNDER-STOOP!

OHHH!! HUGE!!
YOTSUBA-CHAN, PUT YOUR BICYCLE OVER HERE.
WE CAN'T RIDE THEM IN THERE.
WHAT ABOUT MIURA?
I'M ALLOWED.
BECAUSE I'M A PRIN-CESS.
OH, OKAY!

DO YOU WANT TO TRY TOO, YOTSUBA?
...
YEAH!
I WANNA TRY!

YOTSUBA&!

YOTSUBA&!

FEVER

#44

SORRY TO KEEP YOU WAITING.
THANKS.
ぼた
BOTA (PLOP)
ぼた
BOTA
HMM.
THERE'S MORE WHERE THAT CAME FROM!
ずっ
I'LL GO GET IT!

SFX: ZU (SIP)

*ROE: FISH EGGS, COMMONLY USED IN SUSHI.

*AN APPROXIMATE CONVERSION IS ONE U.S. DOLLAR TO 100 YEN.

MAKING MILK IS HARD?
IT'S A LOT HARDER TO MAKE GOOD MILK THAN BOTTLED WATER.
YOTSUBA WANTS TO MAKE MILK.
YOU'VE BEEN SAYING THAT...
MILK TASTES BESTEST WHEN JUST MADE!
RIGHT?
YOTSUBA, DO YOU KNOW HOW MILK IS MADE?
UMM...
COWS...
RIGHT?
OH, COWS, HUH?
AND WHAT DO YOU DO WITH THE COWS?

YOU SQUEEZE THEM.
SQUEEZE!
...SQUEEZE THE WHOLE COW?
I DON'T KNOW
DON'T KNOW!
ばん
BAN (BAM)
がしゃん
GASHAN (G'SKRASH)
どん
DON (THWUMP)
URGH!
COFFEE MILK IS FROM BLACK COWS?
AH—
AND REGULAR MILK WOULD COME FROM WHITE COWS?
THEN WHAT ABOUT STRAW-BERRY MILK?
THERE AREN'T ANY RED COWS, YOU KNOW?
HMM...
THAT'S BLOOD!
COW'S BLOOD!
THAT'S A SCARY THOUGHT.

HAAA! HAAA!
はなれてみる
NOTE: DON'T SIT TOO CLOSE.
DADDY! GIMME A PIGGY-BACK RIDE!
DADDY! GIMME A PIGGY-BACK RIDE!
UHHH...
HUP
OH! I'M ALMOST AS TALL AS JUMBO NOW!
JUMBO HAS A BIG FACE!!
THE ONLY WAY TO SETTLE THIS NOW IS WITH A STARING CONTEST!

LET'S ALL GO TO A RANCH TOMORROW.

A RANCH!?
GET DOWN FOR A MINUTE.
JUMBO, ARE YOU FREE TOMORROW?
YEAH, I CAN GO.
WHAT RANCH SHOULD WE GO TO?
A RANCH !?
A RANCH, WHERE COWS ARE!?
WE'RE GOING TO COWS' PLACE!?
YUP, IT'S THE COWS' PLACE WHERE COWS ARE.
A RANCH!!

YAAAY!
GRILLED BEEF!?
GRILLED BEEF!?
YOU WANNA GRILL THEM?
!?
?
WELL ...
IF WE'RE GOING TO GO, YOU SHOULD BE GETTING TO BED NOW, YOTSUBA.
TIME TO CALL IT A NIGHT.
I DON'T WANNA GO TO BED!
I WANNA PLAY WITH JUMBO MORE!
YOU DIDN'T HAVE A NAP THIS AFTERNOON. NOW LET'S GO RIGHT TO BED.
I DON'T NEED A NAP!
JUMBO, LET'S FIGHT!
NOOO! LET'S PLAAAY!
JUMBO'S GOING HOME SOON.
WHAT ARE YOU DOING?
LET'S PLAY RANCH! JUMBO, YOU BE THE COW!

URRNN—
ZU (SLIDE)
ずっ
ZU
ずっ
JA (SHAK)
じゃっ
AHH, NICE WEATHER.

DADDY, YOU'RE UP.
LET'S GO TO THE RANCH.
OKAY, BUT FIRST WE EAT BREAK-FAST...
YOU'RE ...

101.3°F.
AH.
I'M FINE.
NO, YOU'RE NOT.
THE TRIP TO THE RANCH IS CANCELLED.
YOU NEED TO STAY IN AND REST TODAY.

NO
WAY—!!
GO TO THE RANCH! GO TO THE RANCH! GO TO THE RANCH! GO TO THE RANCH! GO TO THE RANCH!
RANCH! RANCH! RANCH! RANCH! RANCH! RANCH! RANCH! RANCH! RANCH! RANCH! RANCH! RANCH! RANCH! RANCH! RANCH! RANCH! RANCH! RANCH! RANCH!
RANCH! RANCH!

I'M OKAY! I'M OKAY, SO LET'S GO!
YOU'RE NOT OKAY.
THIS IS WHY I TOLD YOU TO GO RIGHT TO BED YESTERDAY.
THIS HAPPENED BECAUSE YOU DIDN'T LISTEN TO WHAT I SAID.
FROM NOW ON!
I'LL GO RIGHT TO BED FROM NOW ON!
SFX: PURURURURU (BRIIIING) PURURURURU
I'LL LISTEN TO WHAT YOU SAY...
WHERE YOU CALLING?
THE RANCH, TO MAKE A RESERVATION?
プルルルル
プルルルル
YEAH, JUMBO?
WELL ...
UH, IT'S YOTSUBA.
SHE HAS A FEVER.

YEAH. SO I'M CALLING OFF THE TRIP TO THE RANCH.
GYAAAAAH!!
AAAAAAAH!
AAAAAAAAH!
AAAAAAAAAH!
AAAAAAAAAAAH!
AAAAAAAAAH!
AAAAAAAAAH!
AAAAAAAAAH!
YOTSUBA, GET BACK IN YOUR BED.
I DON'T WANNA!!
AAAAAAAAH!

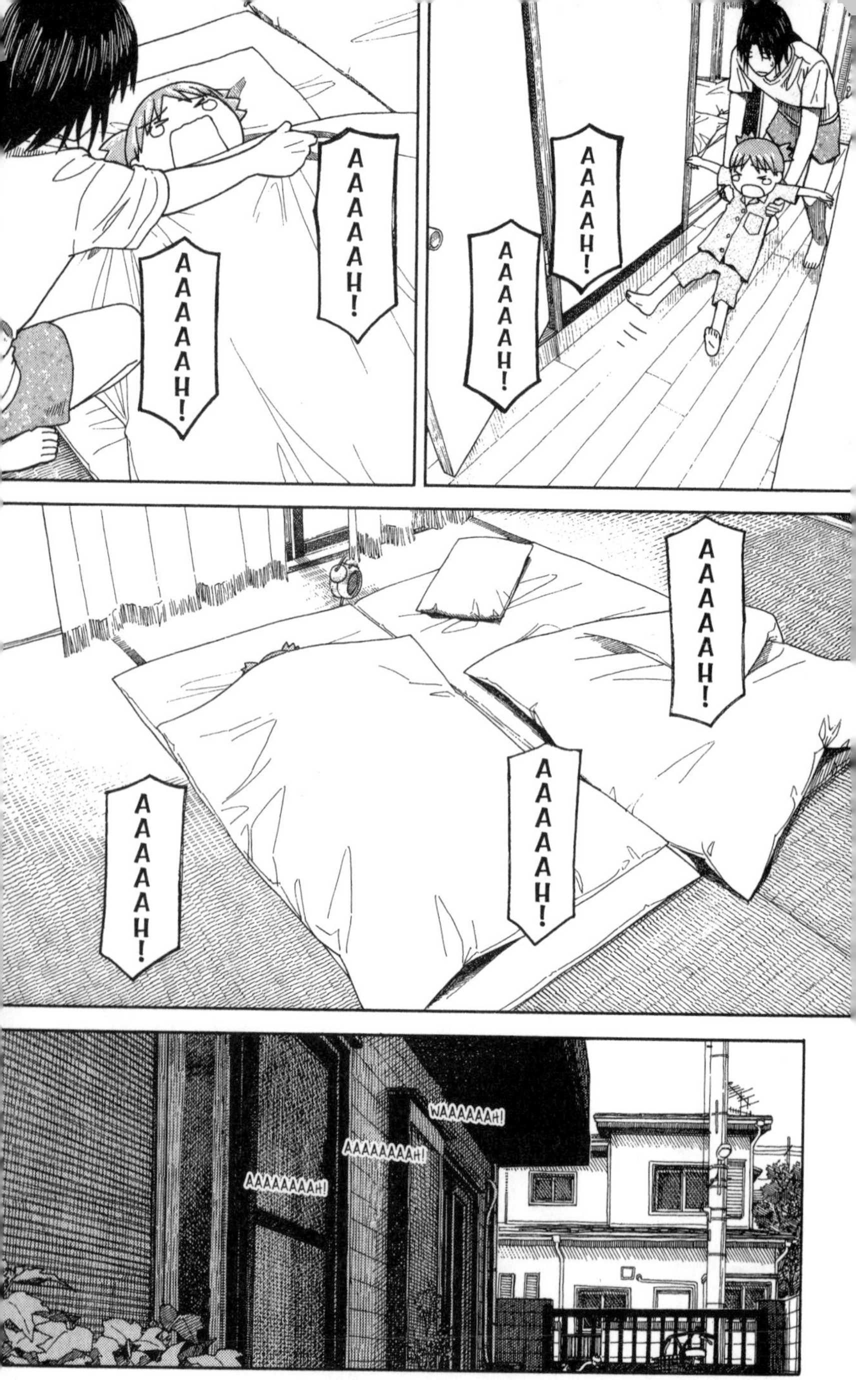
AAAAAH!
AAAAAAH!
AAAAAAH!
AAAAAAH!
AAAAAAH!
AAAAAAH!
AAAAAAH!
WAAAAAAAH!
AAAAAAAAAH!
AAAAAAAAAH!

AAAAAH!
AAAAAH!
AAAAAH!
AAAAAH!
YOTSUBA, WE'LL GO TO THE RANCH SOME OTHER TIME.
SOME OTHER TIME NO GOOD.
GO TODAY.

LOOK, IF YOU REST ALL DAY TODAY, YOUR FEVER WILL PROBABLY BREAK.
IF YOU STILL HAVE A FEVER TOMORROW, WE'LL GO TO THE DOCTOR'S.
...
...WILL I GET A SHOT?
YEAH, PROBABLY.
BUT YOU DON'T MIND GETTING A SHOT, DO YOU?
......
YES, I DO.
THEN GET SOME REST.
AS A SPECIAL TREAT, I'LL LET YOU REST IN THE TV ROOM TODAY.
!
REALLY!?
THAT'S SPESHAL...
?
OKAY, HANG ON TO YOUR BLANKETS.
HUP.

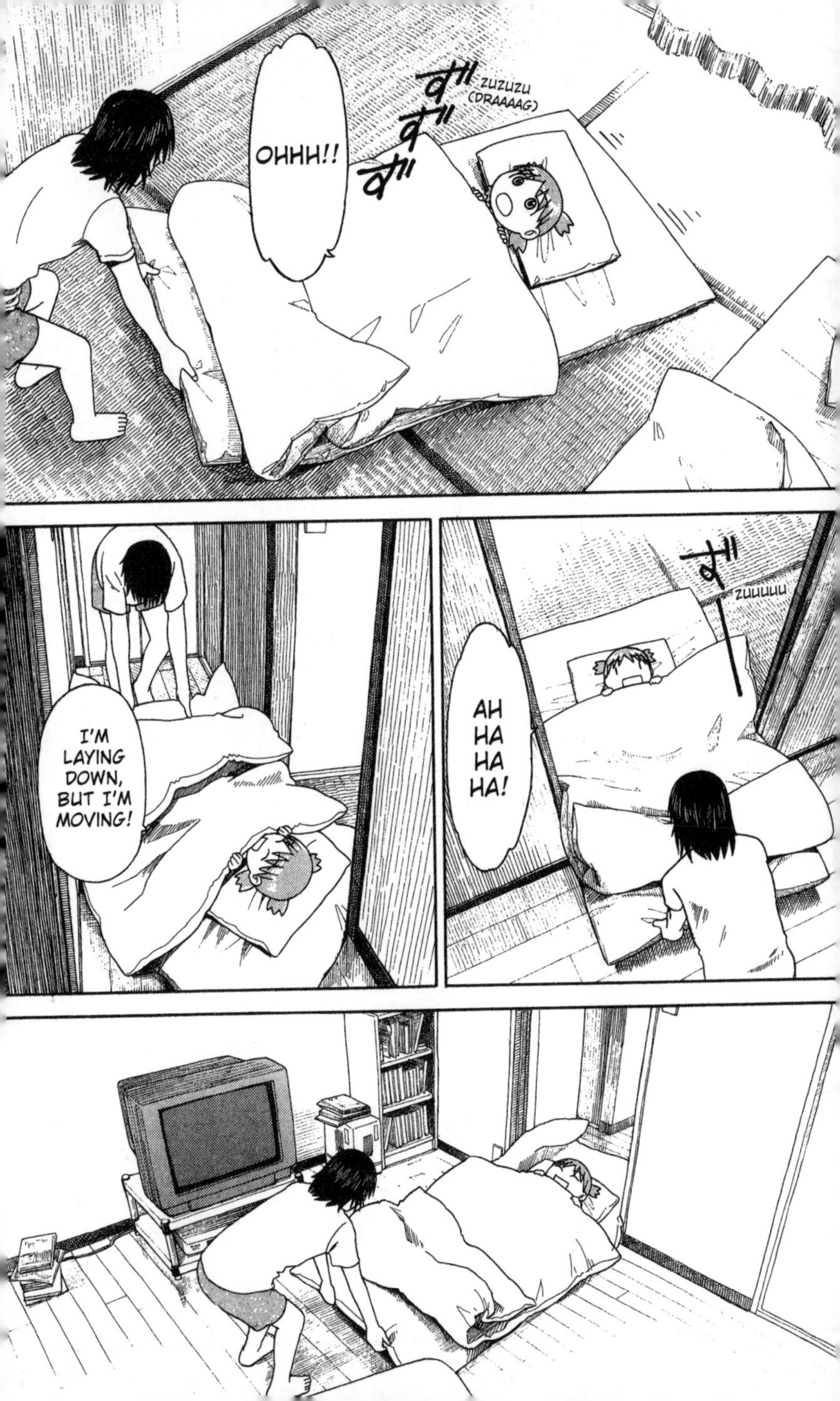
ずずず
ZUZUZU (DRAAAAG)
OHHH!!
ず
ZUUUUU
AH HA HA HA!
I'M LAYING DOWN, BUT I'M MOVING!

HERE YOTSUBA, PUT THIS COLD WRAP ON YOUR FOREHEAD.
ぺたっ
PETA (STICK)
COLD!
DADDY...
...I WANNA WATCH MORE OF THE VIDEO WE BOUGHT.
OKAY.
JUST A MINUTE.

BLUE
YOTSUBA WANTS TO GO THERE WITH DADDY.
HN?
THE SOUTH POLE, HUH?
IT'S COLD THERE. REALLY, REALLY COLD.
OKAY.

AUGN...
URRNN...
GOOD.

DADDY, TURN THE TV ON.
IT'S OFF.
OH, YOU'RE UP?
HERE, DRINK SOME WATER.
OKAY.
IT'S NICE AND COOL TODAY.
WE HAVEN'T EVEN HAD TO USE THE A/C LATELY.

I GUESS I WON'T BE ABLE TO SIT AROUND IN JUST MY BOXERS FOR MUCH LONGER...
PUT ON PANTS, DADDY.
YOU'LL CATCH A COLD.
...YOU'RE RIGHT.
...NAH, I'M GOING TO HOLD OUT FOR A LITTLE BIT LONGER.
I SEE ...

*ONIGIRI: A JAPANESE FOOD TYPICALLY MADE OF WHITE RICE PACKED INTO A TRIANGLE SHAPE AND WRAPPED IN SEAWEED WITH A SAVORY FILLING, LIKE SALTED FISH.

ONIGIRI, HUH? OKAY, LET'S GO WITH THAT.
BUT NO UMEBOSHI.*
HUH? BUT YOU CAN'T HAVE ONIGIRI WITHOUT UMEBOSHI.
YOU DON'T LIKE UME-BOSHI, HUH?
EVERYBODY MAKES A WEIRD FACE WHEN THEY EAT UMEBOSHI, SO IT'S SCARY.
HUH!?
THAT'S WHY!?
*UMEBOSHI: A SOUR PLUM OFTEN FOUND IN ONIGIRI
UURGH!
LIKE THAT.
UURGH!

OTSUBA&!

YOTSUBA& THE PÂTISSIER!

#45

ぱっ
PA
(PAT)
GUESS WHO?
!?
WHO IS IT!?
FUUKA!?
OH!? OH!?
BZZZT!
ASAGI!
BZZZT!
ENA!? MOM!?
BZZZT! BZZZT!

WHO ARE YOU!?

HEH HEH HEH.
I KNOW YOU, YOTSUBA-CHAN.
YOU LOVE MILK.
!
HOW DID YOU KNOW...?
ARE YOU A SPY ...?
A MILK LADY...?
YOU REALLY DON'T REMEMBER ME, DO YOU?
WE MET WHEN YOU WENT TO THE SCHOOL LAST TIME.
!
OHHH!
FUUKA'S BUDDY!?
WELL, I GUESS YOU COULD SAY THAT.
BUDDY...

HUH?
MISS STAKE, YOU AND YOTSUBA ARE ALREADY FRIENDS?
YEAH.
SO WE CAME TOGETHER.
MISTAKE?
MISS STAKE.
IT'S MY NICK-NAME.
MY REAL NAME IS HIWATARI.
MISS STAKE.
MISS STAKE.
CAN WE GET STARTED SOON?
YEAH, I'VE GOT EVERYTHING READY.
MIS-TAKE!

WHY IS FUUKA DRESSED LIKE THAT?
PLAYING SHEFF? GONNA MAKE HAM-BURGER?
I'M NOT MAKING HAM-BURGERS.
AND I'M NOT REALLY A CHEF, I'M MORE LIKE...
A PÂTISSIER!
PATISSEER!?
WHAT'S THAT!? HAM-BURGER!?
IT HAS NOTHING TO DO WITH HAM-BURGER.
A PÂTISSIER IS SOME-ONE WHO MAKES SWEETS.
AND TODAY I'LL BE MAKING A CAKE!
CAKE!!
FUUKA CAN MAKE CAKE!?

YES.
I THINK.
GASHI (GRAB)
I LOVE FUUKA!
SHE CONFESSED HER FEELINGS FOR ME!
JUST GO AHEAD AND START DATING, WHY DON'T YOU?
ARE YOU REALLY GOING TO BE MAKING CAKE?
YAY! ENA-CHAN!
WHY ARE THEY HUGGING?

OUR CLASS IS GOING TO BE DOING A SHOP FOR THE CULTURE FESTIVAL.
WE WANT TO TRY SELLING CAKE, SO...
...WE'RE PRACTICING FIRST.
WOW—
WHAT KIND OF CAKE ARE YOU GOING TO MAKE?
HEH HEH.
THIS!
WE'RE GOING TO MAKE THIS!
OHHH! YOU CAN MAKE THIS!?
OHHH!
CON-GRATS!!
?

IT'S STRAWBERRY SHORTCAKE.
BUT WE'RE MAKING POUND CAKE FOR THE FESTIVAL, RIGHT?
WE HAVE TO START WITH THE BASICS.
STRAWBERRY SHORTCAKE IS PRETTY BASIC.
IT SEEMS SIMPLE ENOUGH.
AND BESIDES, I LIKE IT.
WHO CARES?
YOU SHOULD HAVE SOME WHEN WE'RE FINISHED, ENA-CHAN.
YAAAY!
YOTSUBA WILL HAVE SOME TOO!
FUUKA-ONEECHAN DOESN'T NORMALLY MAKE CAKE, SO DO YOUR BEST, MISS STAKE.
THIS IS MY FIRST TIME TOO.
BUT I'LL DO MY BEST.
OH, I SEE.
IT'S MY FIRST TIME TOO, BUT LEAVE IT TO ME.
YOTSUBA'S FIRST TIME TOO, BUT YOTSUBA LOVES CAKE!
HERE, LOOK AT THIS BOOK. THE CAKE INSTRUCTIONS FIT ON ONE PAGE.
YOU'RE RIGHT. LOOKS EASY.
EASY, RIGHT?
I'M NOT SO SURE...

OKAY! THEN YOTSU-BA'LL MAKE IT TOO!
OH? CAN YOU DO THAT?
YOTSU-BA'LL MAKE THE CAKE WITH YOU!
YOTSUBA WANNA WEAR THIS COOK DRESS TOO.
YOU MEAN THE APRON?
THIS.
THEN YOU CAN BORROW MINE.
MY SCHOOL APRON.
ENA HAS ONE TOO?
HUH?
WHAT?

IT'S A SHEFF HAT!
SO COOL!
WHY DO YOU HAVE SOME-THING LIKE THAT?
UH, I JUST THOUGHT I'D GET INTO THE SPIRIT...
...SO I BOUGHT IT...
I WAS GOING TO BUY A 35 CM HIGH ONE, BUT I THOUGHT THAT MIGHT BE OVERKILL, SO I BOUGHT A 20 CM ONE.
...YOU DON'T SAY...
...I'LL LET YOTSUBA-CHAN BORROW IT.
OHHH!!
MIS-TAKE'S A NICE GUY!
PUT THIS ON TOO, AND YOU'LL LOOK SO COOL.
ALL RIGHT! TIME TO MAKE SOME DELICIOUS CAKE!
YEAH!
YEAH!
MAKE IT A GOOD ONE, OKAY?

TOP BOX: YOTSUBA BUTTER (YEP, IT'S AN ACTUAL BRAND!)

GAN (WHACK)
SFX: GUCHA (GSKRACK)
SHE'S REALLY GOING AT IT!
GAN
AAAH—
NOW I FEEL LIKE I'M REALLY BAKING.
I THINK I MIGHT JUST BE CUT OUT TO BE A PÂTIS-SIER.
HEH HEEEH. ♪
KASHA KASHA (KSHK)
KASHA KASHA
IT SAYS TO BEAT IT TOGETHER UNTIL IT TURNS WHITISH.
IT TURNS WHITISH?
AH.
HEY! NO EATING OUT OF THE BOWL!
YUMMY.
REALLY?
IT'S SWEET.

カシャ KASHA
カシャ KASHA
カシャ KASHA
カシャ KASHA
カシャ KASHA
カシャ KASHA
UMM... I THINK ...
I JUST REALIZED THIS TAKES A LOT OF HEAVY LABOR.
IT'S NOT MIXED AT ALL YET.
IT'S LIKE, DON'T UNDERESTIMATE WHAT IT TAKES TO BE A PÂTISSIER.
YOTSUBA'LL DO IT TOO!
WHY DON'T WE ALL TAKE TURNS AND DO IT?
NEXT TIME I'LL BUY A HAND MIXER.
IT SAYS TO MIX IT UNTIL IT FLUFFS UP TO TWICE WHAT IT WAS IN THE BEGINNING.
WE'RE NOT EVEN CLOSE.
HARDER! HARDER, YOTSUBA-CHAN.
LIKE THIS? LIKE THIS?
日清
日清
フラワー

NOT DONE YET... I GUESS. IT DOESN'T LOOK VERY MIXED AT ALL...
IT DOESN'T LOOK LIKE THE PICTURE IN THIS BOOK.
MY ARM HURTS.
OW.
OW.
OUCH.
OUCH.
OUCH.
OW.
OW.
OUCH.
BUT THE PAIN WE FEEL RIGHT NOW WILL MAKE THE CAKE TASTE JUST THAT MUCH BETTER.
OH.
HARD AT WORK, HUH?

HUH? WHY AREN'T YOU USING A HAND MIXER?
I WOULD IF WE HAD ONE.
WE DO.
HUH?
ギョワー
GYOWAAA (WHRRRRR)
WOW! WOW!
LOOK! LOOK! IT'S *MIXING!*
ギョオオオ
GYOOOO
YOTSU-BA'LL DO IT!
YOTSU-BA'LL DO IT!
BUT GOING THROUGH PAIN MAKES THE CAKE TASTE BETTER.
I'D RATHER *NOT* GO THROUGH PAIN *AND* HAVE IT TASTE GOOD.

NOW WE JUST BAKE IT FOR A WHILE.
IF ALL GOES WELL, IT'LL PUFF UP NICE AND BIG.
WOW.
SFX: NGOOOOOO (VRRRRRRNNN)
!
BA (BWP)
WHAT ARE YOU DOING?
UH, THE CREATION DANCE.
WE NEED SOMETHING TO REMEMBER THIS BY.
OOH, I GET IT.
THEN LET'S TRY TO EXPRESS THE DELICIOUSNESS, SWEETNESS, AND BITTER-SWEETNESS OF THE CAKE IN A DANCE.

WHAT DOES THAT EXPRESS, MISS STAKE?
AS THE CAKE RISES, OUR DREAMS GROW WITH IT.
OHHH.
WHY IS MISTAKE MISTAKE?
DID YOU MAKE SOME KIND OF MISTAKE?
UMM...
WHEN I INTRODUCED MYSELF AT SCHOOL...
...I MESSED UP AND SAID ...

*IN JAPANESE, MISS STAKE MISSPOKE, CHANGING THE LAST WORD OF THE STANDARD INTRODUCTORY GREETING "YOROSHIKU ONEGAI SHIMASU" TO "SHIMAU." ADDING "SHIMAU" TO THE END INDICATES SOMETHING WAS DONE BY MISTAKE, WHICH IS WHERE SHE GETS HER NICKNAME FROM.

GYAUGH!
UMM... DOESN'T IT LOOK KIND OF... WITHERED? IT DIDN'T REALLY RISE...
HMM, MAYBE IT'LL LOOK BETTER WHEN WE PUT THE WHIPPED CREAM ON IT?

OKAY, I'LL SPREAD IT ON.
MAKE IT LOOK NICE.
HEH-HEH-HEH. JUST TRUST MY SENSE OF AESTHETICS.
DON'T ASK THE IMPOS-SIBLE.
PETA (DAB)
PETA
BETA (PASTE)
BETA
BETA
BETA
DOESN'T LOOK RIGHT, HUH?
THIS STINKS...
IT'S GETTING WEIRDER AND WEIRDER...
THE WHIPPED CREAM WAS PROBABLY HARD.
MISS STAKE, YOU TAKE OVER.
OKAY. JUST LEAVE IT TO ME!

......
SEE?
DOESN'T LOOK RIGHT.
I CAN JUST HEAR ASAGI AND MOM LAUGHING AT ME RIGHT NOW!
ENA TOO!?
THIS DEFINITELY HAS A LITTLE TOO MUCH OF THAT HOME-MADE FEEL.
...I KNOW. WE'LL LET YOTSUBA-CHAN DO THE DECORATING.
AH.
OHHH! LEAVE IT TO YOTSU-BA!
べったべったべった
BETTA (SLATHER)
BETTA
BETTA

*POCKY: THIN, BISCUIT-LIKE STICKS, MOST OFTEN DIPPED IN CHOCOLATE.

GA (SMOOSH)
OHHHH!
PERFECT!!
IT LOOKS REALLY GOOD!
I WAS WORRIED FOR A WHILE THERE.
HOW'D IT TURN OUT?
NOW, LET US EXPRESS WHAT WE'RE FEELING RIGHT NOW.

OOH...
SO THEY'RE MAKING A CAKE, HUH? I CAN'T WAIT TO TASTE IT.
I JUST HEARD SOMEONE SAY, "IT'S FINISHED!"

YOTSUBA&!

!
ゲラゲラゲラ
GERA (CACKLE)
GERA
GERA

OH, YOU'RE HERE?
I DID SAY, "HELLO? ANYONE HOME?"
amazon.co.jp
WHAT'S WITH THAT?
ぱち
PACHI (BLINK)
OH, SHE'S UP.

GORON
(ROLL)
!
NGU
(CHEW)
NGU
GAAAAAH!!
HUH!? WHAT'S THAT SUP-POSED TO BE!?
MIS-SILE!
YOU DON'T KNOW MISSILE!?
YOU SHOOT MISSILES OUT OF YOUR MOUTH?
THEY'D BURN YOU TO A CRISP!
YOTSUBA'S GOING TO A RANCH ON THURSDAY!
HUH!?
END OF CON-VERSA-TION!?

YO-TSUBA'S GOING WITH DADDY AND JUMBO.
RIGHT?
YEAH.
AW, COME ON, GO ON SUNDAY. I HAVE WORK ON THURSDAY.
SFX: ZUUUU (SLUUUURP)
SIGH—
I WANNA GET OUT MORE.
I KNOW, I'LL GO TO HAWAII. YEAH, HAWAII.
HAWAII ALREADY WENT TO MIURA!
HA HA HA!
REALLY? DANG. MIURA ALREADY WENT, HUH?
... MIURA?
GAAAAH!
!?

YOTSUBA&
ERRANDS
#46

BUUUU (VROOOM)
フゥウゥゥ
WE SHOULD HAVE LUNCH NOW TOO.
YEAH!
HYAA!
HYAA!
INSTANT RAMEN! WE HAVE INSTANT RAMEN TODAY!
UHH ...
I HAVEN'T HAD IT IN A LOOOONG TIME, SO IT'S OKAY!
BUT WE DON'T HAVE ANY IN THE HOUSE.
YOTSU-BA'LL GO BUY SOME!
I'LL BUY SOME FOR DADDY TOO, WHILE I'M AT IT!

GOING ON AN ERRAND IS HARD! IT MIGHT TURN OUT LIKE THAT TV SHOW "MY FIRST ERRAND."
YOU'LL GET LOST AND TRIP AND FALL AND CRY...
AH HA HA!
I'M NOT LIKE THAT KID!
WELL, THE CONVE-NIENCE STORE IS CLOSE, AND THE WAY IS SAFE...
CONVE-NIENCE STORE.
I KNOW.
I CAN GO.
...OKAY THEN, MAYBE I'LL ASK YOU TO GO ON A LITTLE ERRAND.
YES, SIR!

I LIKE MY RAMEN TO BE SPICY.
WHICH ONE IS SPICY?
HMM ...
IF YOU PICK OUT A RED ONE, IT'LL PROBABLY BE SPICY.
THE RED ONES ARE SPICY, HUH?
I'M GOING TO STOP EATING RED THINGS.
BUY ME AN ERASER TOO.
UNDERSTAND?
I UNDERSTAND!
OKAY, I'LL GIVE YOU ¥500.
DON'T DROP IT!
OKAY!
AND BRING BACK MY CHANGE.
OKAY!
500

TURN AT THAT CORNER AND GO STRAIGHT.
DON'T GO WANDERING OFF.
AND DON'T RUN. WALK.
I UNDER-STAND PER-FECT!
SEE YOU LATER!
ARE YOU SURE YOU CAN DO THIS ...?
HEY!! I THOUGHT I TOLD YOU NOT TO RUN!!
DA (DASH)

HERE WE GO!
GAAA (GSSSSHHH)
WEL...
...COME.
THANKS!

I'LL BUY RAMEN.
BECAUSE I'M A CUSTOMER.
THIS. I TAKE THIS.
ALMOST MISSED IT.
RAAAMEN
RAAAMEN.
IT'S A MONKEY!

は
AH!
RAMEN!
LOTS OF RAMEN!
WHOA.
WITH SO MANY, EVEN IF I EAT ONE A WEEK...
...I COULD EAT ONE EVERY DAY...
THERE' A RED ONE!
THAT ONE'S RED TOO.
AND THAT ONE TOO.
THAT ONE'S A LITTLE RED TOO.
MY MOTHER TOLD ME...
...TO PICK THE VERY BEST ONE AND YOU ARE...
IT!
PACKAGE: TANUKI
IT'S NOT RED!

OH.
THIS IS RED.
IT'S A GOOD RED.
CH-
-I-
-LI
PEP-
-PER
CHILI PEPPER!
PACKAGE: CHILI PEPPER NOODLES VERY SPICY
HMM.
'SCUSE ME!
HUH!?
YES?
DADDY LIKES THE SPICY ONES.
THE RED ONES.
YOTSUBA DOESN'T LIKE THE SPICY ONES.
THE SPICY ONES ARE RED.
THIS IS FOR...
... DADDY.
IS THIS SPICY?
UM...
YES, I THINK THAT'S PRETTY SPICY.
YEAH.
ABOUT FIVE?
FIVE?

WHICH ONE SHOULD YOTSUBA HAVE?
AH.
... 'SCUSE ME.

自然素材
WOULD YOU LIKE ME TO WARM UP YOUR LUNCH?
YES.
HMM.
WHAT ARE YOU LOOKING FOR THIS TIME?
SOME-THING LONG.
?
SOME-THING LONG?
?
ABOUT HOW LONG?
...ABOUT THIS LONG.
HMM.
Lotion Tissue

LIKE THIS ...?
A FLUORESCENT LIGHT BULB?
?
AH!
THAT! THAT'LL WORK!
THANKS!
?

ぎゅ
GYU (SHOVE)
ぎゅっ
GYU
NEXT IS...
WHAT WAS NEXT?
NEXT IS...

CHOCO BABY
CHOCO BABY
CHOCO BABY
PACKAGE: MILK CARAMEL
BOX: SANDWICH COOKIES
UP!
WAS IT CANDY ...?
IT WAS CANDY!

HMM ...
WHICH ONE?
PACKAGE: CHOCO BALLS
THAT WILL BE ¥105.

I DON'T NEED A BAG.
THEN I'LL PUT THIS STICKER ON.
THANK YOU VERY MUCH.
HNN...
WELCOME.
ARE YOU ON AN ER-RAND?
YUP!
ALL BY YOUR-SELF?
YUP!
WOW, I'M SO PROUD OF YOU!
HOME RUN!
?
PACKAGE: CHOCO BALLS
PI (BEEP)

OKAY, YOUR TOTAL IS ¥576.
500
HUH?
IS THAT ALL THE MONEY YOU HAVE?
YOU DON'T HAVE ANY MORE?
THIS IS ALL OF DADDY'S MONEY.
OH, DEAR.
THEN YOU'RE A LITTLE SHORT.
CLOSE, BUT YOU'RE OUT.
!?
CHANGE, PLEASE.
UMM...
YOU DON'T HAVE ENOUGH MONEY.
YOU CAN'T BUY ALL OF THIS.

HMM, WHAT SHOULD I DO...
...YOU DON'T UNDER-STAND AT ALL.

500
CUP NOODLE
I'M GOING HOME.
NO, NO, HOLD IT RIGHT THERE!
IF YOU GO HOME NOW, YOU'LL REGRET IT FOR THE REST OF YOUR LIFE!
!?

IF YOU GIVE UP JUST ONE OF THESE, YOU CAN BUY ALL OF THE REST.
!
REALLY!? WHICH ONE SHOULD I GIVE UP!?
IT DOESN'T MATTER. PICK ANY ONE TO TAKE OUT.
WHICH ONE OF THESE DO YOU LIKE THE LEAST?
PACKAGE: CHILI PEPPER NOODLES
THIS ONE.
OKAY, THEN, LET'S TAKE THAT ONE OUT.

OKAY, THIS MINUS THAT MAKES IT...
...¥376.
I CAN BUY THEM?
YOU SURE CAN.
I'LL EVEN TOSS IN A BUNCH OF CHOP-STICKS FOR FREE.
WOW!
HERE'S YOUR CHANGE.
AND YOUR RECEIPT.
WOW!
THANK YOU.
WHAT ABOUT MY STICKER?
HUH? STICKER?

BYE-BYE, STRANGE LADY!

OH.
I'M HOME!

HOW DID IT GO? DID YOU BUY EVERY-THING LIKE I ASKED?
YUP! I BOUGHT IT JUST LIKE YOU ASKED!
WOW, YOU DID BETTER THAN I THOUGHT.
GOOD JOB, YOTSUBA.
YAY——!!

AH.
がさ
GASA (RUSTLE)
がさ
GASA
WHAT? YOU BOUGHT CANDY TOO?
YUP! I BOUGHT IT JUST LIKE DADDY TOLD ME!
WHAT AM I GOING TO DO WITH YOU?
ぐにー
GUNII (PINCH)
AH HA HA HA HA!
OKAY THEN, LET'S EAT OUR RAMEN TOGETHER.
OKAY!

YOTSUBA&!

CALENDAR
CALENDAR: RANCH
URNN—

I WOULDN'T BE SURPRISED IF A NEW LIFE-FORM STARTED GROWING IN THERE.
......
I GUESS WE'LL ORDER TAKE-OUT.
HEY!
YOTSUBA, ABOUT DINNER...
GUUU (SNOOORE)

SHE'S SLEEPING ALREADY?
PACHI (BLINK)
パチッ
OH.
MUKU (SHF)
ムク
HEY, YOTSUBA ...
TIME TO GO TO THE RANCH!
LET'S TAKE OFF!
WE'RE NOT TAKING OFF ANYWHERE.
WE'LL BE GOING TO THE RANCH TOMOR-ROW.
!?
WHAT!?

*UDON: THICK WHEAT FLOUR NOODLES.

ふ ふ
SFX: FUUU (FOOO) FUUU
FIVE! SIX! SEVEN!
YOU SLEPT TOO MUCH THIS AFTERNOON.
CAN'T SLEEP!

AAAUGH...
YEAH, IF YOU DON'T GET TO SLEEP SOON, YOU'LL GET A FEVER AGAIN.
I HAVE TO SLEEP... I HAVE TO GET TO SLEEP SOON...
HOW...
UURRGH, HOW DO I SLEEP?
KUUU (SNOOORE)
SHE GOES TO SLEEP FAST.

IT'S MORNING!
WE OVER-SLEPT!
GABA (SHWP)
DADDY! IT'S MORNING! WAKE UP!
WE OVER-SLEPT!
UUUGH... WHAT TIME IS IT?
I DON'T KNOW!?
JA (SHAK)

YOTSUBA&
TAKING OFF
#47

がらっ
SFX: GARA (CLATTER)
GOOD MORNING, MR. BIRD.
ガー
GAAA (CAW)
CAAAAAW!!
バサッ
BASA (FLAP)
IT'S A NICE, COOL MORNING!

YAWN ...
OH, YOU'RE RIGHT. WE OVERSLEPT A LITTLE.
HAA!
GO GET READY, YOTSUBA.
OKAY!
WASHA (BRUSH)
WASHA
WASHA
WASHA
BRUSHING OUR TEETH COMES AFTER WE EAT BREAK-FAST, WRONG?
WE'RE GOING TO BE EATING BREAKFAST ON THE WAY.

WE EAT BREAK-FAST OUT TOO?
YEAH!
KIND OF EXCITING, ISN'T IT?
PUE (PTOOEY)
ぷえ
KODOMO USAGI
OKAY!
ALL READY!

I'M READY TO GO.
I'M GOING.
SEE YOU LATER.
HOLD ON, HOLD ON.
DID DADDY FINISH WORK?
WILL YOU BE OKAY IF YOU GO TO THE RANCH?
YEAH, I FINISHED. IT'S OKAY.
YOU WORKED VERY HARD! I'M PROUD!
THANK YOU VERY MUCH.
ピンポーン
PIN POON (DING-DONG)
JUMBO'S HERE!
だだ DA (THD)
だ DA
だッ DA
JUMBO!!

YO.

BAN!
(SLAM)
KODOMO
USAGI
カチャ…
KACHA
(KCHAK)
ガ
GA
(GSH)
そ〜
SO
(PEEK)
!

HEH HEH HEH.
YOU CAN'T CLOSE IT NOW!
GYAAAAAH!!
WHY ARE YOU HERE...?
KODOMO USAGI
DON'T COME!
DON'T COME!
WAAAAAH!
DADDY!
DADDY!

MORNIN'!
THANKS FOR SEEING US OFF.
OKAY, LET'S GO, YOTSU-BA.
NO, WAIT!

I WANT TO GO TOO.
NOBODY ASKED YOU.
DON'T YOU HAVE TO WORK? PLAYING HOOKY?
I TOOK A VACATION DAY.
I DON'T TAKE MANY DAYS OFF, SO I'VE GOT A BUNCH OF THEM NOW.
I WORKED ON MY DAY OFF THE DAY BEFORE YESTERDAY TOO.
HMM.
YOTSUBA, YANDA SAYS HE WANTS TO GO TOO.
WHAT DO YOU THINK, YOTSUBA?
LET'S GO TO THE RANCH TOGETHER, YOTSUBA!
N. O.

HUH!?
WHY NOT!?
WHY'D YOU SPELL IT OUT?
COME ON, YOTSUBA. THE MORE THE MERRIER!
YEAH, HE'S RIGHT. THE MORE THE MER-RIER.
EVEN IF IT'S YANDA?
ANSWER HER, ALREADY!
IT'LL BE FUN! CRAZY FUN!

WILL YOU LISTEN TO YOTSUBA TODAY?
I WILL! I WILL! YOU BET I WILL!
THEN WE CAN BRING HIM AS SPESHAL TREAT.
YOU'RE SO NICE, YOTSUBA.
YOTSUBA WAS NICE.
OKAY THEN.
LET'S TAKE OFF!
HEY!!
WAH!
HUH!?

YO-TSUBA SAYS "LET'S TAKE OFF"!
HUH? WHY?
THAT'S THE RULE!
THE RULE, HUH?
FOLLOW THE RULE, YANDA!
SORRY.
GOOD.
LET'S ...
... TAKE OFF!

YOTSUBA SITS IN FRONT!
YAAAY!
I LIKE THE FRONT TOO!
YAAAY!
GU (GLARE)
ぐ

SHAAAAA!!

WELL, THAT DECIDES IT...
YUP.
HUH!? DECIDES WHAT!?
HMPH.
HUH!? WHY!?
YOU GETTING IN OR NOT? WE'LL LEAVE YOU BEHIND.
WE'LL LEAVE YOU BEHIND.
I'M GETTIN' IN!
I'M GETTIN' IN!

THIS IS THE FIRST TIME I'VE RIDDEN IN THIS CAR.
WOW, THE STEERING WHEEL'S ON THE LEFT? THAT'S PRETTY BRASH FOR A FLORIST'S BRAT.
SHUT UP. THIS WAS ALL THEY HAD WHEN I BOUGHT IT.
I LIKE THE STEERING WHEEL ON THE RIGHT.
DADDY, I'M HUNGRY.
HOLD ON A LITTLE LONGER.
YOU'RE HUNGRY ALREADY? THAT CAME OUT OF NOWHERE.
WE HAD NO BREAKFAST.
HUH? HE DIDN'T FEED YOU?
DID YOU DO SOMETHING BAD?
WE'RE ALL GOING TO EAT AT A SERVICE AREA.
YOTSUBA HAD UDON FROM HINODEYA YESTERDAY.
WHO ASKED YOU?
BUT HINODEYA'S HANDMADE, SO IT'S GOOD, ISN'T IT?
YOTSUBA HAD CROQUETTE UDON.
HOW MUCH LONGER 'TIL WE CAN EAT?
WE'LL BE AT THE SERVICE AREA IN ABOUT THIRTY MINUTES.

*COW DAY: THE MIDSUMMER DAY OF THE OX (OR COW), CALLED DOYOU USHI NO HI, IS SUPPOSED TO BE THE HOTTEST DAY OF THE YEAR.

JUMBO! IS THAT WHERE YOU PAY THE MONEY!?
YOU PAY THE MONEY WHEN YOU LEAVE. THIS IS WHERE YOU TAKE THE TICKET.
THE TICKET!
YO-TSUBA WANTS TO TAKE IT!
THIS BOOTH DOESN'T HAVE E.T.C.,* RIGHT?
NO. OKAY, YOTSUBA. GO AHEAD AND TAKE IT FOR ME.
OHHH!
*E.T.C.: ELECTRONIC TOLL COLLECTION
SIGN: TAKE TICKET
通行券を
お取り下さい
通行券を
お取り下さい
TAKE TICKET
OH! PAPER CAME OUT!
YEAH. TAKE IT FOR ME.

通行券を
お取り下さい
TAKE TICKET
AAAAAAAH!!
!?
TAKE TICKET
DON'T WORRY, YOU CAN TAKE IT.
STOP MESSING AROUND.
!?
IT'S OKAY. GO AHEAD AND TAKE IT.
I'M SERIOUSLY GONNA THROW YOU OUT!

ONE DAY, IN THE FOREST ...
...I DIDN'T MET A BEAR...
...I MET A COW...
WHAT THE HECK?

YOTSUBA& THE RANCH

#48

AH!
LOOK AT THE HUGE MOUNTAIN!
YAHOOO!

YANDA IS STUPID.
WHAT ARE YOU GOING TO THE RANCH TO DO, YOTSUBA?
WE'RE ALMOST AT THE RANCH.
RANCH HAS COWS.
LISTEN UP, AND I'LL TELL YOU.
WHAT'S WITH THE CONDE-SCENDING LOOK?
I HAVE TO EXPLAIN EVERY LITTLE THING TO YOU?
I HAVE TO START FROM THE BEGIN-NING?
YOU LITTLE BRAT...
HUH!? THAT'S IT!?

COWS ARE...
... CUTE!
HUH? NO WAY!
THEY'RE BLACK AND WHITE!!
WHAT ARE YOU TALKING ABOUT?
COWS ARE HUGE, THEY'RE NOT CUTE!!
WHY CAN'T THEY BE HUGE AND CUTE, HUH!?
I WASN'T TALKING TO YOU!!
WHAT DOES DADDY THINK!?
I THINK COWS ARE CUTE.
DON'T GIVE ME THAT SMUG LOOK!

YO-TSUBA THINKS COWS ARE CUTE TOO!
LISTEN TO ME WHEN I'M SPEAKING! YOU GET OUT OF THIS CAR!
WE'RE HERE!
SIGN: RANCH
SIGN: WELCOME

WOOW...
SO THIS IS IT...
THIS HOUSE IS THE RANCH!?
THERE'S COWS IN THERE?
NOT JUST THE HOUSE ...
THIS WHOOOLE AREA IS THE RANCH.
ALL OF IT!?
THE WHOLE THING!?
I THINK SO.
CAN WE JUST GO IN?
AH!
THERE!
COME ON, GUYS!
YEAH!!

IT'S A CAT!
A CAT!?
IT'S CUTE, ISN'T IT?
CUTE.
CUTE.
GUNI (RUB)
GUNI
GUNI
GUNI
DA (DASH)
AH! IT RAN AWAY!
ALL RIGHT! AFTER IT!
WHO CARES ABOUT A CAT!?
HUH!?
COME ON, GUYS!
Y-YEAH!

DAN
(THMP)

ANIMALS!!
SHEEP!
YEAH. THOSE ARE SHEEP.
IT LOOKS LIKE WE CAN GO IN.
DA (DASH)

YOTSUBA, THIS IS A HILL, SO DON'T RUN OR YOU'LL FALL!
IT'S OKAY!

AH.

KORO (ROLLL)
KORO
KORO
KORO
DON (THUD)

MAN, SHE REALLY ROLLED!
AH HA HA HA!
ROLL-ROLL-ROLL! AH-HA-HA-HA-HA!
SFX: GERA (CACKLE) GERA GERA
NOW LOOK.
YOU SCARED THEM, AND THEY RAN AWAY.
AWWW...
!?
YOTSUBA WILL APOLOGIZE TO THE SHEEP AND MAKE UP WITH THEM.
YOU WILL? OKAY THEN, GO AHEAD.

HEEEY! SHEEP!
I FELL, SO I COULDN'T HELP IT.
DON'T BE SCARED ANY MORE, ALL RIGHT?
LET'S BE FRIENDS, OKAY?
DON (THUD)
GORO GORO (ROLL)
ZASHAA (ZSKSSSHH)
YOTSUBA!!

GO (WHAM)
GAAAAAAH!!
STOP IT!!
KODOMO USAGI
I THOUGHT I TOLD YOU AT THE ZOO NOT TO PUNCH THE ANIMALS.
HE STARTED IT!
ARE YOU HURT?
SHE PUNCHED ANIMALS AT THE ZOO?
THIS GUY'S STRONG.

WHAT ARE THEY ALL EATING?
HORSE-TAIL?
AH! GRASS!
THEY'RE EATING GRASS!
HOW CAN THEY EAT GRASS?
WELL, THAT'S JUST HOW THEY ARE.
...I DO WONDER HOW THEY CAN DO THAT, THOUGH ...
SFX: ZUZUZU (SLIIDE)
ズズズ
OOH!
YOTSUBA, DIG YOUR HANDS INTO THE SHEEP'S WOOL.
OHHH!
THEY GO FAR IN!
THIS WOOL IS USED TO MAKE THINGS LIKE SWEATERS AND CARPET.
WOW! THEY'RE USEFUL!

THESE ONES ARE GOATS.
THEY'RE ALWAYS EATING.
I LIKE GOATS BETTER THAN SHEEP.
THEY'RE CUTE.
WHAT ARE GOATS USEFUL FOR?
GOATS ARE...
HMM, I WONDER WHAT THEY USE THESE GOATS FOR...
FUR? MEAT?
GOAT'S MILK?
BUT I HAVEN'T SEEN ANY BEING SOLD.
HEY, GOAT. WHAT ARE YOU USEFUL FOR?
ARE YOU MAKING YOURSELF USEFUL AT THIS RANCH?
GET TO WORK, GOAT.
DON'T TEASE HIM! DON'T TEASE THE GOAT!

INFORMATION
COFFEE & MILK TICKET
SIGN: EXPERIENCE COW MILKING, EVERY DAY 11:00 A.M., EVERY DAY 1:00 P.M., PRICE PER PERSON ¥700
乳しぼり体験
1回目 11時00分
2回目 13時00分
料金 お一人様 700円
※ソフトクリーム付き
お申込みのお客様はINFORMATIONまで
OKAY, LET'S DO THIS.
... MILKING ...?
SIGN (CONT.): *ICE CREAM INCLUDED, INTERESTED PERSONS SHOULD GO TO THE INFORMATION WINDOW
FRONTIER HO
EXCUSE ME.
EXCUSE COW MILKING!
WHAT ARE YOU TALKING ABOUT?
IT SAYS, "EXPERIENCE COW MILKING"! YOU GET TO DO WHAT THE RANCH HANDS DO AND MILK A COW!
IT'S A DOG! THERE'S A DOG TOO!
WHOSE HOUSE IS THAT?
THIS IS THE COWS' HOUSE.
OHHH, THIS IS WHERE THEY LIVE...

UM, EXCUSE ME.
YOU'RE HERE FOR THE COW MILKING, RIGHT?
COULD YOU WAIT JUST A MOMENT? I'M GETTING EVERYTHING READY.
CAN I GO INTO THE COWS' HOUSE?
SURE. GO RIGHT AHEAD.
OH!
OH!

WHOA! THEY'RE HUGE!
YEAH, THEY'RE BIGGER THAN I THOUGHT.
COWS ARE HUGE!

WHOA THERE.
WAAAAH!
WHAT ARE YOU DOING!?
WHAT, YOU'RE NOT AFRAID OF COWS, ARE YOU?
THEY'RE CUTE, RIGHT?
I'M NOT AFRAID!!
YOU'RE SCARED.
I AM NOT SCARED!!
WHY, YOU LITTLE LIAR.
KYUU (PINCH)
DON'T GRAB MY NOSE!!
AH-HA-HA-HA! HER VOICE SOUNDS SO NASAL!
YEAH, I GUESS IT WOULD...
OKAY, IF YOU'RE NOT AFRAID, THEN PROVE IT.
I'LL PROVE IT!

GU (CLENCH)
WAH!! DON'T PUNCH IT!!
I GOT THE POINT!! YOTSUBA, I GOT THE POINT!!
I GOT YOUR POINT, YOTSUBA. YOU'RE NOT AFRAID.
THESE GUYS MIGHT LOOK LAID-BACK, BUT THEY'LL PUT UP A FIGHT, SO WATCH OUT.

THERE, THERE.
IT'S NOISY IN HERE, HUH?
DADDY! LOOK! I TOUCHED IT!
OH? HAVE YOU GOTTEN USED TO IT NOW?
PERON (LICK)
I'M ALL READY! RIGHT THIS WAY, PLEASE.

FOUR PEOPLE, RIGHT?
LINE UP, LINE UP!
?
ONE!
DO IT! DO IT RIGHT!
HUH? OH, YEAH...
ONE!
TWO!
THREE!
FOUR!

FIVE!
HUH —!?
YOTSUBA, FIVE IS WRONG.
WHAT ARE YOU TRYING TO DO?
HUH!?
OKAY, I'LL EXPLAIN HOW TO MILK A COW.
OKAY!
ZAN (ZWP)
WHAT —!?

PRETEND MY THUMB IS THE UDDER.
FIRST, YOU GRAB THE TOP PART OF THE UDDER TIGHTLY WITH YOUR THUMB AND INDEX FINGER.
AND THEN, YOU COUNT TO FIVE...
...SQUEEZING THE UDDER EACH TIME.
THEN YOU RELAX YOUR HAND AND DO THE SAME THING AGAIN.
I UNDER-STAND!
YOTSUBA CAN COUNT TO FIVE, SO SHE UNDER-STANDS!
I'M SO PROUD OF YOU!
I CAN COUNT TO FIVE TOO, SO I UNDER-STAND TOO.
I CAN COUNT TOO. I UNDER-STAND.
I CAN COUNT TOO. I UNDER-STAND.
I- I'M SO PROUD OF YOU.
I'M FIVE!
GREAT!

OOH.
IT'S WARM.
1, 2, 3, 4, 5...
HUH?
SQUEEZE THE VERY TOP PART TIGHT.
YOU CAN SQUEEZE IT HARDER.
SQUEEZE IT QUICKLY.
ちゃ
SFX: CHAAA (FSSSHHT)
IT CAME OUT!
DADDY, I DID IT!
OHHH!
OHHH!

AH HA HA HA!
IT'S JUST LIKE MILK.
WHAT ARE YOU TALKING ABOUT? THAT IS MILK.
YANDA, YOU BE QUIET!
YO-TSU-BA.
THAT'S MILK.
!
WHAT? REALLY!?
WHAT DOES JUMBO THINK!?
THAT'S MILK.
PERO (LICK)
AH!
THERE'S MILK IN THERE!
WHO MADE IT!? WHO PUT IT IN THERE!?
UMM...
THE COW MADE IT HERSELF. SHE SAVED IT UP IN THERE HERSELF.
THE COW DID...?

PACHI (CLAP)
PACHI
PACHI
PACHI
PACHI
PACHI
PACHI
YOU GUYS TOO!
YOU GUYS CLAP FOR THE COW TOO!
UH, O-OKAY.
PACHI
PACHI
PACHI
PACHI
PACHI
PACHI
PACHI
PACHI

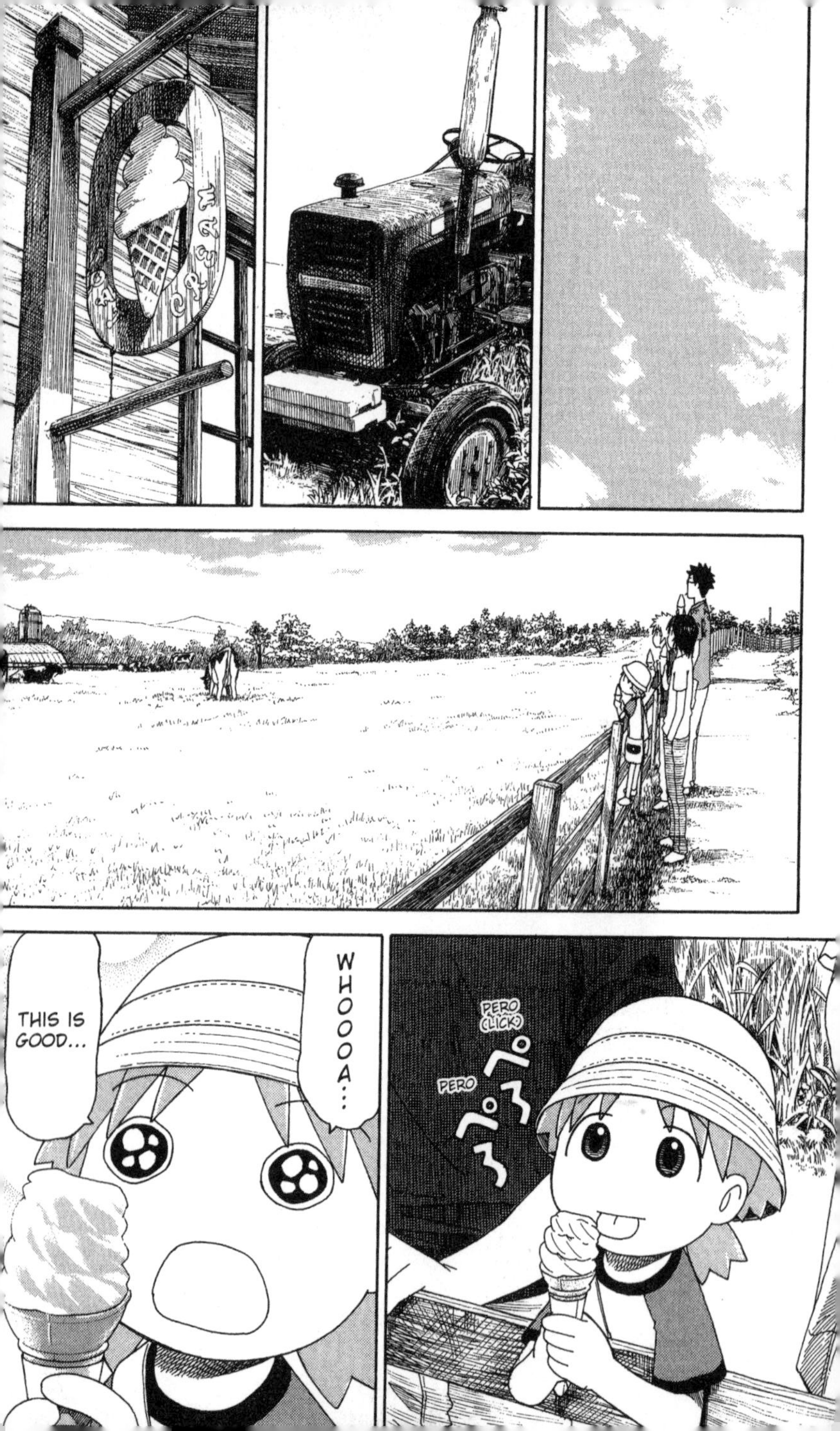
WHOOOOA...
THIS IS GOOD...
PERO (LICK)
PERO
ぺろ
ぺろ

IT FEELS LIKE LIGHT IS SHINING OUT OF MY MOUTH.
...WHAT DOES THAT MEAN?
YOTSUBA, DO YOU KNOW WHAT ICE CREAM IS MADE OUT OF?
......
YEAH, I KNOW!
OH?
THEN WHAT IS IT MADE OUT OF? PLEASE, TELL ME.
SHELL-FISH.
BISHI (BWSH)

IT'S SHELL-FISH.
SURE.
JUMBO-SAN, PLEASE TELL THIS KID THE RIGHT ANSWER!
YUP, SHELL-FISH.
IT'S SHELLFISH, RIGHT?
WHAAAA!?
C'MERE.
YOTSUBA, YOTSUBA!
NO, THAT'S WRONG ...
THAT'S WRONG !?

......
......
WHA !?
THE SHELL-FISH WAS A LIE!
IT'S ACTUALLY MADE OUT OF MILK!
WHAAAA!?
TRICKE YOU!
HA-HA-HA-HA-HA!
NO!
YOU DIDN'T TRICK ME AT ALL!!
IN FACT, YOU'RE THE ONE WHO GOT TRICKED!
I DID NOT.
LIAR!
OKAY THEN, WHAT'S BUTTER MADE OUT OF?
AH.
I HAVE TO GIVE THE COWS SOME GRASS.
HEY! LISTEN TO ME!

HERE, PLEASE EAT.
HAVE TO FEED THEM RIGHT SO THEY'LL GROW UP BIG AND STRONG.
THERE, THERE.
BUSY, BUSY!
YOU GOT A BIG FACE.

WHAT'S WRONG WITH BEING BIG!?
I WASN'T TALKING ABOUT YOU!
I'M GOING TO FEED THEM TOO.
WHAT DO YOU THINK, YOTSUBA?
ISN'T THE RANCH FUN?

NOT AT ALL?
HUUUUUUH!?
KOOOMO USAGI
WH-WHY NOT!?
IT'S PRETTY FUN, ISN'T IT!?
HUH!?
WHAT'S WRONG!? DOES YOUR STOMACH HURT!?
A RANCH IS A LOT OF HARD WORK, YOU KNOW!
IT WORKS HARD TO GROW GRASS AND STUFF!
HUH!?
WELL, YEAH, BUT... YOU'RE NOT A RANCH, RIGHT!?
I HAD FUN!
YO-TSUBA HAD LOTS OF FUN!
BUT THAT'S A DIFFERENT STORY!
HUH!? IT IS!?

A RANCH IS A HARD, HARD PLACE—
!?
BECAUSE THERE'S CATS AND SHEEP AND GOATS AND COWS AND—
ICE CREAM— AHH— AHH—
IT'S SO, SO HARD YOU KNOW—
WHY ARE YOU SING-ING?
THE MILK—
THERE'S MORE!? LISTEN TO ME!
AH! A HORSE!
WOULD YOU LISTEN TO WHAT YOUR OWN DAUGHTER IS SINGING!?
A HORSE !?
YOU MEAN, YOU MEAN...

THAT KIND OF HORSE !?
THAT KIND OF HORSE!
OKAY! LET'S GO!
YEAH!!

YOTSUBA&! 7

KIYOHIKO AZUMA

Translation: Amy Forsyth
Lettering: Terri Delgado

Yen Press
Hachette Book Group
237 Park Avenue, New York, NY 10017

www.HachetteBookGroup.com
www.YenPress.com

Yen Press is an imprint of Hachette Book Group, Inc. The Yen Press name and logo are trademarks of Hachette Book Group, Inc.

First Yen Press Edition: December 2009

ISBN: 978-0-316-07325-7

10 9 8 7 6 5 4 3 2 1

BVG

Printed in the United States of America

YOTSUBA&!

ENJOY EVERYTHING.

TO BE CONTINUED!